Pharo with Style

Stéphane Ducasse

March 6, 2022

Copyright 2022 by Stéphane Ducasse.

The contents of this book are protected under the Creative Commons Attribution-NonCommercial-NoDerivs CC BY-NC-ND
You are free to:

Share — copy and redistribute the material in any medium or format

The licensor cannot revoke these freedoms as long as you follow the license terms. Under the following conditions:

Attribution. — You must give appropriate credit, provide a link to the license, and indicate if changes were made. You may do so in any reasonable manner, but not in any way that suggests the licensor endorses you or your use.

NonCommercial. — You may not use the material for commercial purposes.

NoDerivatives. — If you remix, transform, or build upon the material, you may not distribute the modified material.

No additional restrictions. — You may not apply legal terms or technological measures that legally restrict others from doing anything the license permits.

https://creativecommons.org/licenses/by-nc-nd/4.0/legalcode

Any of the above conditions can be waived if you get permission from the copyright holder. Nothing in this license impairs or restricts the author's moral rights.

Keepers of the lighthouse
Édition : BoD - Books on Demand,
12/14 rond-point des Champs-Élysées,75008 Paris
Impression : BoD - Books on Demand, Norderstedt, Allemagne
ISBN: 9782322182015
Dépôt légal : Mars 2022
Layout and typography based on the sbabook LaTeX class by Damien Pollet.

Contents

1 General naming conventions   3
1.1 Guideline: Favor simple direct meaning 3
1.2 Guideline: Use descriptive names 3
1.3 Guideline: Pay attention to meaning 4
1.4 Guideline: Follow domain 5
1.5 Guideline: Favor unique meaning and pronunciation 6
1.6 Guideline: Limit or use abbreviations consistently 6
1.7 Guideline: Avoid numbers 6
1.8 Conclusion 7

2 About class names   9
2.1 Guideline: Use direct and natural style 9
2.2 Guideline: Use natural language 10
2.3 Guideline: Do not expose implementation 10
2.4 Guideline: Avoid to use plural for class names 11
2.5 Guideline: Avoid name collisions 11
2.6 Guideline: Class names should indicate the class' parent 11
2.7 Conclusion 12

3 About identifier format   15
3.1 Guideline: Avoid underscores and favor camel case 15
3.2 Guideline: CamelCase fully identifiers 16
3.3 Guideline: Shared variables start with uppercase 16
3.4 Guideline: Private variables start with lowercase 17
3.5 Guideline: Convey language semantics 17
3.6 Guideline: Method selectors start with lowercase 18
3.7 Conclusion 18

4 About variable names   21
4.1 Guideline: Favor semantic variables 21
4.2 Guideline: Use typed variables to indicate API 22
4.3 Guideline: Get the best from semantic and type variable 23
4.4 Guideline: Use semantics for state variable 23
4.5 Guideline: Use predicate for Boolean 24

4.6	Guideline: Use common nouns and phrases	24

5 About method names   25

5.1	Guideline: Choose selectors to form short sentences	25
5.2	Guideline: Use imperative verbs for actions	25
5.3	Guideline: Prefix selector with as for conversion	26
5.4	Guideline: Indicate flow with preposition	26
5.5	Guideline: Indicate returned type	27
5.6	Guideline: Use interrogative form for testing	28
5.7	Guideline: Avoid using parameter and variable name type	28
5.8	Guideline: Use accessors or not	29
5.9	Guideline: Name accessors following variable name	29
5.10	Guideline: Avoid return in lazy blocks	30
5.11	Guideline: Avoid prefixing setters with set	31
5.12	Guideline: Use basic or raw to access low-level	31
5.13	Guideline: Follow conventions and idioms	31
5.14	Guideline: Distinguish between class and instance selectors	32
5.15	Guidelines: Follow existing protocols	34

6 About code formatting   35

6.1	Guideline: Be consistent	35
6.2	Guideline: Use the general method template	36
6.3	Guideline: Indent method body	37
6.4	Guideline: Separate signature and comments from method body	37
6.5	Guideline: Use space to give breath to code	38
6.6	Guideline: Align properly	39
6.7	Guideline: Use tabs not spaces to indent and use spaces to help reading . . .	39
6.8	Guideline: Do not break lines randomly	40
6.9	Guideline: Highlight control flow	41
6.10	Guideline: Declare temporary close their use	42

7 Comments   43

7.1	Guideline: Method comments	43
7.2	Guideline: Good comment do not paraphrase code	44
7.3	Guideline: Use active voice and short sentences	45
7.4	Guideline: Include executable comments	45
7.5	Guideline: Use CRC-driven class comments	46
7.6	Guideline: Comment the unusual	47

8 Powerful coding idioms   49

8.1	Guideline: Do not query twice for the same object	49
8.2	Guideline: Move return outside branches	49
8.3	Guideline: Use streamContents	50
8.4	Guideline: Preallocate overly large collections	50
8.5	Guideline: Use super to send a message with the same selector	51

9 Object initialization — 53
- 9.1 Guideline: Take advantage of automatic object initialization — 53
- 9.2 Guideline: No automatic initialize — 54
- 9.3 Guideline: No double super new initialize — 54
- 9.4 Guideline: initialize does not need to return super — 55

10 Potential traps: A syntactic perspective — 57
- 10.1 Guideline: Use parentheses to disambiguate messages with the same priority — 57
- 10.2 Guideline: no need for extra parentheses — 58
- 10.3 Guideline: receiver of ifTrue:ifFalse: is a boolean — 60
- 10.4 Guideline: receiver of whileTrue: is a block — 61
- 10.5 Guideline: Use a Block when you do not know execution time — 61
- 10.6 Guideline: Avoid , when in loop — 62
- 10.7 Guideline: super is just self — 63
- 10.8 Guideline: Do not reuse temporaries — 63
- 10.9 Guideline: Do not change behavior of well-known messages — 64
- 10.10 Guideline: Use iterators — 64
- 10.11 Guideline: Avoid low-level messages — 64
- 10.12 Guideline: Do not abuse blocks — 64
- 10.13 Guideline: Do not write lengthly blocks — 65
- 10.14 Guideline: Exception catch MUST not be empty — 65

11 Potential traps: About printing and Streams — 67
- 11.1 Guideline: `printString` vs. `displayString` — 67
- 11.2 Guideline: About `printString` — 68
- 11.3 Guideline: Unnecessary stream creation — 69
- 11.4 Guideline: `printString` vs. `asString` — 70

12 Use Patterns — 71
- 12.1 Guideline: Write small methods — 71
- 12.2 Guideline: Avoid singletons — 71
- 12.3 Guideline: Avoid explicit Transcript — 72
- 12.4 The real concern — 73
- 12.5 Guideline: Parametrized your object with log stream — 74
- 12.6 When instance creation is delicate — 74
- 12.7 Guideline: Wrap explicit signal raising — 76

13 Conclusion — 77

Contents

Programming is a lot more than just writing algorithms or programs. Programming is all about communication. Communication with others: not only with the other programmers who will be involved in your development effort, but also with yourself. Indeed, finding good names is a really important task because using the right name often opens the door to new spaces where your design can bloom and expand.

The purpose of a programming style guide such as this book is to provide a simple vehicle for addressing the needs of good communication. The goal is to make the source code clear, easy to read, and easy to understand and extend.

These conventions are not cast in stone, but they set the foundation of a common culture. Culture is important when programming.

We were influenced by the excellent little book called *Smalltalk with Style*. We hope that you will enjoy this one and that it will help you become a better communicative designer.

Feedback and suggestions are welcome at stephane.ducasse@inria.fr.

Pull requests on https://github.com/SquareBracketAssociates/Booklet-PharoWithStyle are also welcome.

Special thank to Réné-Paul Mages, Christopher Furhman, Benoit St Jean and Masashi Fujita, Nathan Reilly, Esteban Maringolo, Hernán Morales for their feedback.

S. Ducasse - 12 February 2022.

CHAPTER 1

General naming conventions

In this chapter, we will start with guidelines about names.

Indeed, names are important. And using *good* names is the cornerstone of writing good software. This is true in any language. We will never repeat it enough.

Now, finding a good name is sometimes difficult. To help, good names are often driven by a domain or an ecosystem. Finally, the object-oriented programming paradigm gives some context that is useful: For example, the "Don't ask, tell" motto favors active and direct orders for method names.

1.1 Guideline: Favor simple direct meaning

Some native English speakers use more precise, but less common terms. Consider that your software may be read by people from different cultures. So use simple, mainstream, and common terms. Note that this does not mean that you should not use precise terms. Avoid hidden or implied meanings that can only be understood by a limited group of people. Make information explicit and clear.

1.2 Guideline: Use descriptive names

Choose descriptive names that capture domain entities unambiguously. Avoid cryptic names. Characters are cheap, so do not count them. If you are slow at typing then use the completion engine.

Prefer
```
dayOfWeek
```
over
```
Not dow
```

Prefer
```
seconds
```
over
```
Not sec
```

Prefer
```
copyMenu
```
over
```
Not cMenu
```

1.3 Guideline: Pay attention to meaning

Pharo uses English as main language. It looks strange to mention it, but this has some implications. We should pay attention to two mistakes that non native english speakers tend to do: first, adjective inversion, and second, keeping the plural form during inversion of composition (using of).

Adjective inversion

Non-English native speakers often misplace word qualifiers (adjective). In English, the qualifier is often before the word it qualifies. In Pharo, we follow such a convention.

Prefer
```
DateParser
```
over
```
Not ParserForDate
```
or
```
Not ParserDate
```

Prefer
```
userAssociation
```

1.4 Guideline: Follow domain

(an association of users)

over

[Not associationUser

No plural inside

In English, the names of methods can also be written method names. Notice that in such a situation there is no s in method.

Prefer

[userAssociation

over

[Not usersAssociation

Avoid homographs

Compare the three following variables:

[sizeToRead
  sizeJustRead
  readSize

In this situation, avoid homographs (https://en.wiktionary.org/wiki/homograph). That is, words that are written the same way but can have different meanings or pronunciations. For example, *Did you read that book? ... Yes, I read it yesterday.* About `readSize`: does this mean that the size was just read (red) or that it is the size to read (reed)?

Favor words with a unique pronunciation.

1.4 Guideline: Follow domain

Follow the domain concepts and culture of the project. Do not invent your own terms because you think they are better. Favor regularity (consistency) over preciseness.

Prefer

[GnatXmlNode

over

[not GNAT_XML_Object

5

When representing the XML Ada abstract syntax tree in Pharo, we should not follow Ada naming conventions. The name should convey that the class is an abstract syntax tree node. Hence, `GnatXmlNode` is much better than `GnatXmlObject`.

Another example is the following: In Moose, an importer is an object creating FAMIX entities (classes, methods, etc.) from the data structure representing a language element, usually an Abstract Syntax Tree (AST). Therefore `GNATInstaller`, which creates entities from an AST, should be renamed `GnatImporter` and `GNATImporter`, which loads an AST in memory should be renamed `GnatASTLoader`.

1.5 Guideline: Favor unique meaning and pronunciation

Choose names that have a unique meaning. Avoid homographs.

Prefer

```
sizeToRead
sizeJustRead
```

over

```
Not readSize
```

Does this mean that the size was just read (red) or is it the size to read (reed)?

1.6 Guideline: Limit or use abbreviations consistently

Abbreviations or acronyms are often obscure to newcomers. Now they are often handy so when you use them use consistently.

Prefer

```
ASTNode
```

over

```
TreeNode
AbstractSyntaxTreeNode
```

1.7 Guideline: Avoid numbers

It can be handy when trying something new to reuse an identifier and add a number to it. Now limit this practice to your development session. Indeed, a number does not help the reader understand the difference. As a general principle, keeping multiple implementations of the same classes is a way to propose rotten code. So if you want to keep several versions then make sure that why several versions are kept is made clear.

Prefer

```
StackBasedInlineParser
NewInlineParser
CleanerInlineParser
```

over

```
InlineParser2
```

1.8 Conclusion

The guidelines presented so far are general. We will see that we also have guidelines for classes and variables.

CHAPTER 2

About class names

In object-oriented programming, classes play an important role. They are factories of objects, and as such, they are important for conveying the main abstractions within an application.

2.1 Guideline: Use direct and natural style

Often, classes represent objects, even abstract ones. Use the names that fit the best without inventing some clunky new terms.

Prefer
```
Terminal
```

over
```
PlaceToDisplayInformation
```

Some classes represent an action (such as Visitor) or process.
```
RBReadBeforeWrittenTester
MicHTMLWriter
```

Finally, some may represent a particular state. In Pharo, announcements follow the convention of finishing with the verb in the past tense. It contradicts English conventions, but it is applied uniformly.
```
IcePackageLoaded
MCVersionSaved
RubBoundsChanged
```

Avoid class name using gerund

$\left[\begin{array}{l}\text{RBParsing}\\ \text{OpeningFile}\end{array}\right.$

2.2 Guideline: Use natural language

When defining class names, avoid abbreviations that are not obvious, avoid shortening names, and favor natural language.

Prefer
$\left[\text{RandomNumberGenerator}\right.$

over
$\left[\text{RandNumbGen}\right.$

Prefer
$\left[\text{CSVImporter}\right.$

over
$\left[\text{CSVImport}\right.$

Prefer
$\left[\text{RemoteControl}\right.$

over
$\left[\text{RemControl}\right.$

Prefer
$\left[\text{Player}\right.$

over
$\left[\text{BoardMan}\right.$

2.3 Guideline: Do not expose implementation

A class name should not expose the implementation the class uses. This is important because implementation may change in the future.

Prefer
$\left[\begin{array}{l}\text{PropertyName}\\ \text{ContactBook}\end{array}\right.$

over

```
PropertyNameString
ContactDictionary
```

2.4 Guideline: Avoid to use plural for class names

A class often has many instances. TestCase classes are special classes where their methods are individual tests. Still, it is really awkward to have a class ending with S.

Prefer
```
AthensTextRenderManualTest
```

over
```
AthensTextRenderManualTests
```

Of course some domain names ends with S, in such as case just follow the convention.

Prefer
```
NetworkSystemSettings
```

2.5 Guideline: Avoid name collisions

To avoid name space collisions, add a prefix indicative of the project to the name of the class.

Prefer
```
PRDocument
CmdMessage
```

> **Note** You may find that Pharo is lacking a namespace. If you have a couple hundred thousand euros, we can fix that!

Note, however, that even with a namespace you will have to pay attention that your namespace name does not collide with another one.

2.6 Guideline: Class names should indicate the class' parent

Suffix class names with the root class to convey the kind of object we are talking about.

For example, without the `Morph` suffix, the reader is forced to check the superclass to understand if the class is about a graphical object or not.

Prefer

```
ClyBrowserButtonMorph
```

over

```
ClyBrowserButton
```

Prefer

```
ClyQueryViewMorph
```

over

```
ClyQueryView
```

Prefer

```
SpLayoutHelpTopics
```

over

```
SpLayouts
```

In the following, not mentioning the `Presenter` suffix makes it unclear to the reader that it is a Presenter object as opposed to a Model object.

Prefer

```
ApplicationWithToolBarPresenter
```

over

```
ApplicationWithToolbar
```

In the next example, `DynamicWidgetChange` does not convey that this is not a *domain* object representing a change, but a `Presenter` object in the Model-View-Presenter triad:

```
DynamicWidgetChangePresenter
```

over

```
DynamicWidgetChange
```

2.7 Conclusion

Finding a good name is often difficult. However, nobody forces you to find it right upfront. And you can always change a name once you find a good one.

A good way to find good names is to write unit tests.

2.7 Conclusion

When you write unit tests, you are the first client of your code. You can then see if the names you chose let you write coherent and comprehensible little stories. You can explore the names you picked up and rename them.

CHAPTER 3

About identifier format

While in the previous chapters we focused on identifiers or class variables, this chapter focuses on the form or format of such names. Indeed, writing software is about writing sentences that seamlessly integrate with existing ones. You do not want your program to be easily identifiable as an existing one. This is particularly true for multiple developer projects with common code ownership. Note that even if you are working on a single-person project, you will use existing class libraries and you do not want to have your 'ugly' code stepping out.

3.1 Guideline: Avoid underscores and favor camel case

The form or format of identifiers is also important. Following the form promoted by a complete ecosystem will make your software more readable and acceptable by others. This is true in any programming language.

Because Pharo and its ecosystem use camel case for class, variable, and method names. Avoid using underscores.

Prefer
```
timeOfDay
```

over
```
timeofday
time_of_day
```

Prefer
```
GnatXmlNode
```

over
```
[ GNAT_XML_Object
```

Prefer
```
[ releasedX
```

over
```
[ released_X
```

Prefer
```
[ | scaledX reducedX |
```

over
```
[ | scaled_X reduced_X |
```

When creating private low-level methods that bind to external C-libraries, you may want to use underscores to follow C conventions to ease tracing back the communication between libraries. In such a case, limit your use to carefully thought-out cases.

3.2 Guideline: CamelCase fully identifiers

Use consistently camel case on the full length of an identifier.

Prefer
```
[ readyForNextItem
```

over
```
[ readyFornextitem
```

3.3 Guideline: Shared variables start with uppercase

Begin class names, global variables, pool variables, and class variables with an uppercase letter. If the word is compound, then use camel case for the rest.

```
Point      "Class"
Transcript "global variable"
PackageGlobalOrganizer   "class variables"
```

3.4 Guideline: Private variables start with lowercase

Begin instance variables, temporary variables, method parameters, and method selectors with lowercase. If the word is compound, then use camel case for the rest.

```
address
classExtensionSelectors
classTags
```

Prefer

```
| dataset f xMatrix scale x |
```

over

```
| dataset f Xmatrix scale X |
```

3.5 Guideline: Convey language semantics

Remember `MaxLimit`, `maxLimit`, `maxlimit`, and `MAXLIMIT` are all different identifiers in Pharo.

```
| MaxLimit maxLimit |
MaxLimit := 10.
maxLimit := 20.
MaxLimit
>>> 10
```

Still, Pharo favors the camel case, so use it systematically for words. Wikipedia defines camel case as: Camel case (stylized as camelCase) is the practice of writing phrases such that each word or abbreviation in the middle of the phrase begins with a capital letter, with no intervening spaces or punctuation.

For local variables.

Method parameters and instance variables, use

```
maxLimit
```

instead of

```
maxlimit
MAXLIMIT
```

For classes, or shared variables

Use

```
OrderedCollection
MaxLimit
```

instead of

```
ORDEREDCOLLECTION
MAXLIMIT
```

> **Note** In a compound word, do not confuse a prefix or suffix with a word when trying to determine which words should begin with an uppercase letter. For example, some readers may think that the "c" in subclass should be uppercase, but sub is a prefix, not a word. When in doubt about prefixes and suffixes, check a dictionary.

Prefer

```
superclass
```

over

```
superClass
```

3.6 Guideline: Method selectors start with lowercase

Prefer

```
getMethodsNamesFromAClass: aClass
  | methodsNames |
  methodsNames := aClass selectors.
  methodsNames do: [ :each | names add: each ]
```

over

```
GetMethodsNamesFromAClass: aClass
  | methodsNames |
  methodsNames := aClass selectors.
  methodsNames do: [ :each | names add: each ]
```

Also, in this example, the method selector is not good because method names are called selectors in Pharo. In addition in English methodsNames should be written methodNames. It should be gatherSelectorsFrom: or something similar.

3.7 Conclusion

This is a bit obvious, but as a developer you should follow language conventions.

3.7 Conclusion

This is not because Pharo is permissive that you should bend the rules. Doing so will only confuse you and other developers. So use camel case. Remember, private or local variables start with a lowercase letter, while class variables start with an uppercase letter.

CHAPTER 4

About variable names

When choosing an appropriate name for a variable, the developer is faced with the decision: *Should I choose a name that conveys semantic meaning to tell the user how to use the variable, or should I choose a name that indicates the type of object the variable is storing?* There are good arguments for both styles. Let us see what the guidelines are that can help us find the right balance.

4.1 Guideline: Favor semantic variables

A semantic name is less restrictive than a type name. When modifying code, it is possible that a variable may change type. But unless one redefines the method, the semantics of it will not change. We recommend using semantically meaningful names wherever possible.

In the example below, the typed variable does not indicate how it will be used, whereas the semantic variable does.

Prefer
```
"Semantic variable"
newSizeOfArray := numberOfAdults size max: numberOfChildren size
```

over
```
"Typed variable"
anInteger := numberOfAdults size max: numberOfChildren size
```

Note that semantic names can convey variable roles. Having more information is definitely useful for clients of the code.

Prefer
```
"Semantic variable"
selectFrom: aBeginningDate to: anEndDate
```

over
```
"Type variable"
selectFrom: aDate to: anotherDate
```

Finding a semantic name is not always as obvious as demonstrated above. There are cases in which choosing a descriptive semantic name is difficult.

4.2 Guideline: Use typed variables to indicate API

Using a type variable is an interesting way to convey the API (set of messages) that the object held in the variable responds to.

Below aDictionary conveys that the argument should have the same API as a Dictionary (at:, at:put:)

Prefer
```
[properties: aDictionary
```

over
```
[properties: map
```

You may also want to stress specific types in an API reference to the interface that the object implements.

Prefer
```
[properties: aPuttable
```

over
```
[properties: aCollection
```

Suppose a String, a Symbol, and nil are valid for a parameter. A developer may be tempted to use the name aStringOrSymbolOrNil.

You may be tempted to aString or anObject. anObject is not really helping the developer who will have to use such variables. At the minimum, such a use should be accompanied by a comment that says, "anObject can be a String or aSymbol"

Some developers may argue that type variables should not refer to classes that do not exist. We disagree. As shown in the following guidelines, it is a lot better to indicate that an argument is a block expecting two arguments (hence a binary block) than to just mention a block. And this works even if there is no binary block class in the system.

Prefer

```
[inject: anObject into: aBinaryBlock
```

over

```
[inject: anObject into: aBlock
```

Note that for `inject:into:` the best naming is to mix semantic ant type naming as in

```
[inject: initialValue into: aBinaryBlock
```

4.3 Guideline: Get the best from semantic and type variable

A good practice is to use a mixture of both semantic and typed variable names. Method parameter names are usually named after their type. Instances, classes, and temporary variables usually have a semantic name. In some cases, a combination of both can be given in the names.

Prefer

```
[ifTrue: trueBlock ifFalse: falseBlock
```

over

```
ifTrue: block1 ifFalse: block2
ifTrue: action1 ifFalse: action2
```

The following are other examples of good names.

```
inject: initialValue into: aBinaryBlock
copyFrom: start to: stop
findFirst: aBlock ifNone: errorBlock
paddedTo: newLength with: anObject
```

4.4 Guideline: Use semantics for state variable

State variable names (instance variables, class variables, or class instance variables) are usually semantic-based. A combination of semantic and type information can be really powerful, too.

Prefer

```
"In class PhoneBook"
phoneNumber
name
```

over

```
number
labelForPerson
```

4.5 Guideline: Use predicate for Boolean

Use predicate clauses or adjectives for Boolean objects or states. Do not use predicate clauses for non-Boolean states.

Prefer
```
alarmEnabled
isAlarmEnabled
```

over
```
alarm
```

4.6 Guideline: Use common nouns and phrases

Use common nouns and phrases for objects that are not Boolean.

```
"In class Vehicle..."
  numberOfTires
  numberOfDoors

"In class AlarmClock..."
  time
  alarmTime

"In class TypeSetter..."
  page
  font
  outputDevice
```

Note that you can also use `count` instead of `numberOf` as in the following example:

```
numberOfTires
tireCount
```

CHAPTER 5

About method names

Method names in Pharo are called selectors. They are used in messages and are the main vehicle to convey adequate meaning to computation. From that perspective, it is really important to use them to convey the exact meaning of the computation they perform. The correct use of words and the design of selectors are then important.

5.1 Guideline: Choose selectors to form short sentences

Choose method names so that someone reading the message can read the expression as if it were a sentence.

Prefer

```
FileDescriptor seekTo: word from: self position
```

over

```
FileDescriptor lseek: word at: self position
```

Write the test first, and make sure that your test scenario reads well.

5.2 Guideline: Use imperative verbs for actions

Use imperative verbs for message which perform an action.

```
transform
    selectors do: [:each | self pushDown: each].
    selectors do: [:each | class removeMethod: each]
```

25

Prefer

`[aReadStream peek]`

over

`[aReadStream word]`

Prefer

`[aFace lookSurprised]`
`[aFace beSurprised]`

over

`[aFace surprised]`

`[skipSeparators]`

Pay attention to the fact that some words can be interpreted as interrogatives, whereas you want to give them an imperative meaning.

For example, compare:

`[optimized]`

and

`[triggerOptimization]`

This is why using `beOptimized` would be better than a simple `optimized` and why `isOptimized` is better for the interrogative form.

5.3 Guideline: Prefix selector with as for conversion

When converting an object to another one, the convention is to prefix the class name of the target with `as`.

`[anArray asOrderedCollection]`

Favor the use of existing classes.

5.4 Guideline: Indicate flow with preposition

When a process state is going from one object to another, indicate the direction using meaningful names.

For example, `flattenProperties:` is not a good name because it does not convey where the properties will be flattened.

`[aConfiguration flattenProperties: aDictionary]`

Better names such as `flattenPropertiesFrom:` and `flattenPropertiesInto:` are much better because there are no ambiguities.

```
aConfiguration flattenPropertiesFrom: aDictionary
aConfiguration flattenPropertiesInto: aDictionary
```

Here are more examples

```
changeField: anInteger to: anObject
```

Prefer

```
ReadWriteStream on: aCollection.
```

over

```
ReadWriteStream for: aCollection.
```

Prefer

```
File openOn: stream
```

over

```
File with: stream
```

Prefer

```
display: anObject on: aMedium
```

over

```
display: anObject using: aMedium
```

5.5 Guideline: Indicate returned type

When a method returns an object (different from the receiver) and this object is not polymorphic with the receiver, it is important to mention it. Since Pharo is not statically typed, we can use the selector name to give such information to the sender of the message.

For example, the method `characterSeparatorMethodSignatureFor:` of the pretty printer did not return a character but a block, as shown below:

```
characterSeparatorMethodSignatureFor: aMethodNode
    ^ [
      (self needsMethodSignatureOnMultipleLinesFor: aMethodNode)
         ifTrue: [ self newLine ]
         ifFalse: [ self space ] ]
```

Favor `characterSeparatorMethodSignatureBlockFor:` over `characterSeparatorMethodSignatureFor:` when the method returns block and not a character as `characterSeparatorMethodSignatureFor:` indicates.

A much better design is to rewrite this method and its users to use a character. Returning a block in such a situation is overkill.

The following method is corresponding to its name.

```
characterSeparatorMethodSignatureFor: aMethodNode
    ^ (self needsMethodSignatureOnMultipleLinesFor: aMethodNode)
        ifTrue: [ self newLine ]
        ifFalse: [ self space ]
```

A good example is the API of the `FileReference` class. The message `pathString` indicates clearly that it returns the path as a string while to access the path object the message `path` should be used.

5.6 Guideline: Use interrogative form for testing

When interrogating the state of an object, use a selector beginning with a verb such as has, is, does,...

Prefer

```
isAtLineEnd
```

over

```
atLineEnd
```

```
aVehicle hasFourWheels
```

over

```
aVehicle fourWheels
```

5.7 Guideline: Avoid using parameter and variable name type

Avoid the parameter type or name in the method name if you are using typed parameter names.

Prefer

```
fileSystem at: aKey put: aFile
```

over

```
fileSystem atKey: aKey putFile: aFile
```

```
"for semantic-based parameter names"
fileSystem atKey: index putFile: pathName
```

```
"useful when your class has several #at:put: methods"
fileSystem definitionAt: aKey put: definition
```

Prefer
```
[aFace changeTo: expression
```

over
```
[aFace changeExpressionTo: expression
```

5.8 Guideline: Use accessors or not

There are different schools about whether to use accessors. In his seminal book, Kent Beck discusses it in depth. Here we give a list of arguments for and against, and you should decide and follow the conventions of the project you work on. In any case, whether you use accessors or not, be consistent.

Arguments in favor of accessors:

- Accessors abstract from the exact state internal representation.
- Accessors may hide that values are derived or not.
- Subclasses may freely redefine the way accessors are implemented.

Arguments against accessor use:

- Accessors expose the internal state of an object.
- When the class is small, using accessors may increase the number of methods.
- Using refactorings, we can always easily introduce accessors.

5.9 Guideline: Name accessors following variable name

When you use accessors, name them consistently:

- The getter is name as the variable it refers to.
- The setter is the same but with an extra terminating colon :.

For getter, prefer
```
tiles
    ^ tiles
```

over
```
getTiles
    ^ tiles
```

Do not use get or set in accessor selectors!

Watch out

Pay attention: a Setter is just setting a value and just returning (implicitly) the receiver. The following setter definition is not correct.

```
BinaryNode >> root: rootNode
    "Set a root node"
    ^ root := rootNode
```

Favor the following one instead:

```
BinaryNode >> root: rootNode

    root := rootNode
```

Note that we do not need to comment a basic setter.

For lazy initialization:

```
tiles
    ^ tiles ifNil: [ tiles := OrderedCollection new ]
```

For setters

```
tiles: aCollection
    tiles := aCollection
```

Put accessors in the 'accessing' protocols. When you have accessors doing extra work place them in a separate protocols to stress their difference.

5.10 Guideline: Avoid return in lazy blocks

You may want to use accessors to implement lazy initialization: the instance variable is initialized only if needed by checking if its value is nil.

Do not place returns inside the block.

Prefer

```
tiles
    ^ tiles ifNil: [ tiles := OrderedCollection new.
```

over

```
tiles
    ^ tiles ifNil: [ tiles := OrderedCollection new. ^tiles ]
```

or even

```
tiles
    tiles ifNil: [ tiles := OrderedCollection new ].
    ^ tiles
```

5.11 Guideline: Avoid prefixing setters with set

Some developers may be tempted to name setter methods by prefixing the variable name

Prefer
```
tiles: aCollection
   tiles := aCollection
```

over
```
setTiles: aCollection
   tiles := aCollection
```

Following K. Beck's advice, use `setTitles:` only for private messages to initialize objects from class side methods.

5.12 Guideline: Use basic or raw to access low-level

When two methods are needed for the same state variable, e.g., one returning the actual stored object and one returning and raising an event, prefix the one returning the actual object with the word `basic` or `raw`.

```
method: aCompiledMethod
   self basicMethod: aCompiledMethod.
   self signal: MethodChanged
```
```
basicMethod: aCompiledMethod
   method := aCompiledMethod
```

When you have a getter that returns an object and a getter that returns a different representation of the same object, add a suffix.

```
path
   ^ path
```
```
pathString
   ^ self path asString
```

5.13 Guideline: Follow conventions and idioms

When designing new objects, you may mimic some of the practices that the system already uses, for example, dictionaries, sets, etc.

Example

Since a style sheet acts as a dictionary of properties, it is much better to use at: instead of get:, especially if you define the message to set a value to a property as at:put: and not set:.

Prefer

```
[stylesheet at: #fontColor
```

over

```
[stylesheet get: #fontColor
```

Prefer

```
[aCollection groupedBy: [ :each | each odd ]
```

over

```
[aCollection groupBy: [ :each | each odd ]
```

Prefer

```
[series at: #k3 put: 'x'.
```

over

```
[series atKey: #k3 put: 'x'
```

Prefer

```
[aCollection at: #toto
```

over

```
[aCollection atKey: #toto
```

5.14 Guideline: Distinguish between class and instance selectors

When defining a class method, we may name it the same way as an accessor of the class. Such practice hampers code readability in the sense that it is difficult to identify rapidly class methods. The senders will report both the instance and class usage. You may think that you will identify the message because the receiver is a class or an instance, but there are many situations where this is not the case. So it's better to enrich the class method with a distinct word.

5.14 Guideline: Distinguish between class and instance selectors

Example

In Pillar, a markup syntax to write documentation, annotations have parameters and the accessor method parameters:. In some versions, an instance creation method with the same name as the accessor method exists.

Reading the code of the parser and in particular the message parameters, it is not clear whether array second is a class or an instance.

```
annotation
  ^ super annotation
    ==>
      [ :array | array second parameters: (array third ifNil: [
    SmallDictionary new ]) ]
```

To create an instance, it is better to name the method newParameter:. This way, we can immediately spot that the second element is a class.

```
annotation
  ^ super annotation
    ==>
      [ :array | array second newParameters: (array third ifNil: [
    SmallDictionary new ]) ]

PRAbstractAnnotation class >> newParameters: aCollection

  | parameters |
  parameters := self checkKeysOf: aCollection.
  ^ self new
    hadAllKeys: aCollection = parameters;
    parameters: parameters;
    yourself
```

is better than

```
PRAbstractAnnotation class >> parameters: aCollection
  | parameters |
  parameters := self checkKeysOf: aCollection.
  ^ self new
    hadAllKeys: aCollection = parameters;
    parameters: parameters;
    yourself
```

Now, if you favor a fluid interface with many parameters, using withParameters: may not be good.

5.15 Guidelines: Follow existing protocols

Protocols are ways to sort methods. It is important to place your methods into adequate protocols since it will ease future exploration of your class.

Pharo provides auto categorisation of protocols for the common methods. So use it as much as possible. If you override your specific methods, place them in similar protocols.

CHAPTER 6

About code formatting

Code formatting improves code comprehension. Readers are used to regular formatting. Don't produce blobs of code. Copy the pros, follow the conventions.

6.1 Guideline: Be consistent

One important guideline when writing code is to follow conventions and, in addition, to be consistent. Systematically apply a formatting style. Keep the violations of conventions to a minimum.

This applies at all levels:

- Class names,
- Method names,
- Instance variable names,
- Method body, and
- Comments.

Inconsistencies will break the reading flow and understanding of the code. Inconsistencies often indicate that different developers touched the code, and they may also be the source of bugs or indicate difficult places in the code.

6.2 Guideline: Use the general method template

- Separate method signature and comments from method body with an empty line.
- Add an extra tab to the comments.
- Add an extra line to stress the beginning of the method body.
- Use a tab to separate the method body from the left margin.

```
message selector and argument names
    "A comment following the guidelines."

    | temporary variables |
    statements
```

For example:

```
addLast: newObject
    "Add newObject to the end of the receiver. Answer newObject."

    lastIndex = array size ifTrue: [ self makeRoomAtLast ].
    lastIndex := lastIndex + 1.
    array at: lastIndex put: newObject.
    ^ newObject
```

Do not let space before the first word of the comment, align comment with method body, make sure that the reader can identify the beginning of the method body by placing an empty line between the method signature and the method body.

Prefer the following

```
collectionNotIncluded
    "Return a collection for wich each element is not included in
        'nonEmpty'"

    ^ collectionWithoutNil
```

over

```
collectionNotIncluded
" return a collection for wich each element is not included in
    'nonEmpty' "
    ^ collectionWithoutNil
```

and over

```
collectionWithoutEqualElements

" return a collection not including equal elements "
    ^collectionWithoutEqualElements
```

6.3 Guideline: Indent method body

Use indentation to convey structure! Do not glue everything on the left margin.

Don't indent your method like this:

```
initialize
super initialize.
symbols := Bag new.
names := Set new
```

Prefer

```
initialize

    super initialize.
    symbols := Bag new.
    names := Set new
```

6.4 Guideline: Separate signature and comments from method body

Separating method comments from the method implementation favor focusing our understanding to the right level. When we want to understand what the method does, we just have to read the comments. When we want to understand how the method is implemented, we just read the method body.

Prefer

```
performCrawling: aName
    "Takes the last word in uppercase as a symbol and eventually add it
       to the bag symbols"

    name := aName copy.
    self getUpperCase.
    self stemSymbolFrom: aName.
    self toUpperCase.
    ^ symbol
```

over

About code formatting

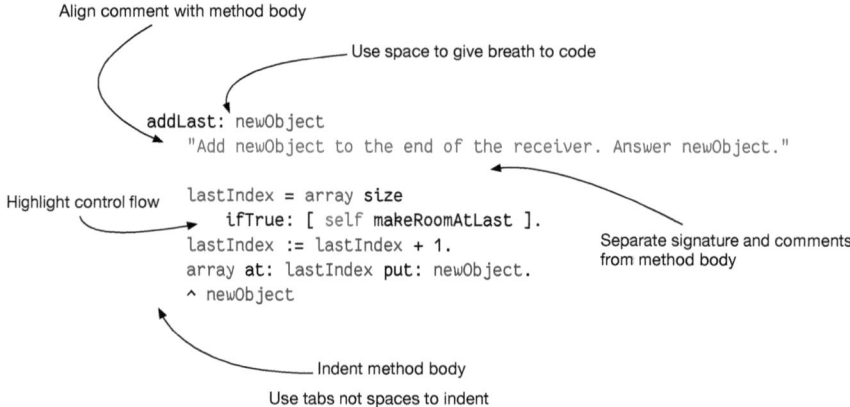

Figure 6-1 A summary of good practices for code.

```
performCrawling: aName
  "Takes the last word in uppercase as a symbol and eventually add it
    to the bag symbols"
  name := aName copy.
  self getUpperCase.
  self stemSymbolFrom: aName.
  self toUpperCase.
  ^ symbol
```

6.5 Guideline: Use space to give breath to code

Gluing all the characters together slows down reading. The reader needs to separate expressions. Gluing characters also hampers the identification of logical groups such as conditional branches.

Put horizontal space to make it easier to read code and clearly identify variables, arguments, assignments, block delimiters and returns.

Prefer

```
stemSymbolFrom: aName

  | stemmer symbol |
  stemmer := SymbolStemmer new.
  symbol := stemmer performCrawling: aName.
  ^ symbol
```

over

6.6 Guideline: Align properly

```
stemSymbolFrom: aName

    |stemmer symbol|
    stemmer := SymbolStemmer new.
    symbol := stemmer performCrawling: aName.
    ^symbol
```

Parentheses do not need spaces (after (and before)) since they show that an expression fits together. But favor space for [and], since they may contain complex expressions.

```
drawOnAthensCanvas: aCanvas bounds: aRectangle color: aColor

    (self canDrawDecoratorsOn: aCanvas) ifFalse: [ ^ self ].
    self drawOnAthensCanvas: aCanvas.
    next drawOnAthensCanvas: aCanvas bounds: aRectangle color: aColor
```

6.6 Guideline: Align properly

Understanding that a piece of code is a coherent expression eases understanding of more complex expressions.

Make sure that your indentation reinforce the identification of block of functionality.

Prefer

```
self phoneBook add:
    (Person new
        name: 'Robin';
        city: 'Ottawa';
        country: 'Canada').
```

over

```
self phoneBook add:
    (Person new
    name: 'Robin';
    city: 'Ottawa';
    country: 'Canada').
```

6.7 Guideline: Use tabs not spaces to indent and use spaces to help reading

When navigating from one element to the next one, spaces and tabs are the same. Since they do not have a visual representation the reader cannot know in advance if the white space in front of word is a tab or multiple spaces. It is then annoying to handle spaces manually.

- Avoid extra spaces at the beginning and use tabs to indent.
- Use one space to separate instructions.
- Avoid extra spaces everywhere: one is enough!
- Avoid extra spaces at the end of the line.

Prefer
```
stemSymbolFrom: aName

    | stemmer symbol |
    stemmer := SymbolStemmer new.
    symbol := stemmer performCrawling: aName.
    ^ symbol
```

over
```
stemSymbolFrom: aName
    |stemmer symbol|
        stemmer:=SymbolStemmer new.
    symbol:=stemmer performCrawling: aName.
     ^symbol
```

6.8 Guideline: Do not break lines randomly

White lines attract the eyes and force the reader to ask himself why the code is separated that way. Only separate method signature and comment from method body with a new line.

Prefer
```
paragraph
    "this method is here to find the paragraph in the chain, instead of
        relying on implementing #doesNotUnderstand: !!!"

    | p |
    p := next.
    [ p isNotNil and: [ p isKindOf: RubParagraph ] ]
        whileFalse: [ p := p next ].
    ^ p
```

over

```
paragraph
  "this method is here to find the paragraph in the chain, instead of
    relying on implementing #doesNotUnderstand: !!!"

  | p |

  p := next.

  [ p isNotNil and: [ p isKindOf: RubParagraph ] ] whileFalse: [
    p := p next.
  ].

  ^p
```

6.9 Guideline: Highlight control flow

Help the reader to understand control flow logic of your code by using indentation.

Prefer
```
size
  "Returns size of a tree - number of nodes in a tree"
  self root isNil
    ifTrue: [ ^0 ].
  ^ self size: self root
```

over
```
size
  "Returns size of a tree - number of nodes in a tree"
  self root isNil
  ifTrue: [ ^0 ].
  ^self size: self root.
```

And prefer
```
depth: aNode
  "Returns depth of a tree starting from the given node"

  | leftDepth rightDepth |
  leftDepth := -1.
  aNode leftChild isNotNil
    ifTrue: [ leftDepth := self depth: aNode leftChild ].
  rightDepth := -1.
  aNode rightChild isNotNil
    ifTrue: [ rightDepth := self depth: aNode rightChild ].
  leftDepth > rightDepth
    ifTrue: [ ^ 1 + leftDepth ]
```

```
      ifFalse: [^ 1 + rightDepth ].
```

over the terribly unreadable `depth:aNode` method.

```
depth: aNode
  "Returns depth of a tree starting from the given node"
  | leftDepth rightDepth |
  leftDepth := -1.
  aNode leftChild isNotNil
  ifTrue: [ leftDepth := self depth: aNode leftChild ].
  rightDepth := -1.
  aNode rightChild isNotNil
  ifTrue: [ rightDepth := self depth: aNode rightChild ].

  ( leftDepth > rightDepth )
  ifTrue: [ ^ (1 + leftDepth) ]
  ifFalse: [^ (1 + rightDepth ) ].
```

6.10 Guideline: Declare temporary close their use

Temporary variables that will only be used within the block should not be defined outside of the block but in the local block.

Prefer

```
| block |
block := [ :arg |
  | local |
  ... local ... ]
```

over

```
| block local |
block := [: arg |
  ... local ... ]
```

CHAPTER 7

Comments

Comments are important. Comments tell readers that they are smart guys and that they correctly guessed your intentions or your code. Do not believe those who claim that methods do not require comments. Obviously, this is what they mean:

1. "Obvious methods" such as accessors do not need comments.
2. A good comment does not describe how the code works in English.
3. It is better to split long methods into smaller ones with a single responsibility,
4. But a good comment is always welcome because it reinforces the understanding of the reader.

A comment should be adapted to the level of granularity (i.e., package, class, or method) to which it applies.

7.1 Guideline: Method comments

Method comments should contain sufficient information for a user to know exactly **how to use** the method, **what** the method does, including any side effects, and **what it answers** without having to look at the source code. Imagine that the source code is not available.

The main method comment is not about its implementation. Do not rephrase the implementation. The second level comments can include information about the implementation. Insert a new line to separate the method comments from the method body.

```
Collection >> asCommaString
    "Return collection printed as 'a, b, c' "
    "#('a' 'b' 'c') asCommaString >>> 'a, b, c'"

    ^ String streamContents: [:s | self asStringOn: s delimiter: ', ']
```

The comments of a method should typically include:

1. the method purpose (even if implemented or supplemented by a subclass)
2. the parameters and their types
3. the possible return values and their types
4. complex or tricky implementation details
5. example usage, if applicable, as a separate comment

Finally accessors do not need comments; the only comment that accessor could have is the purpose of the instance variable.

```
day
    "Answer number of days (an instance of Integer) from
    the receiver to January 1, 1901."

    ^ day
```

7.2 Guideline: Good comment do not paraphrase code

Good Pharo source code is self-documenting, often making comments on statements redundant. Statements need only be commented upon to draw the reader's attention. If the source code implements an algorithm that requires an explanation, then the steps of the algorithm should be commented as needed.

Do not comment on an obvious fact that is expressed simply as plain code.

Prefer
```
| result |
result := self employees
    collect: [:employee | employee salary > amount].
```

over

```
| result |
"Store the employees who have a salary greater than in result."
result := self employees
    collect: [:employee |   employee salary > amount].
```

7.3 Guideline: Use active voice and short sentences

When writing comments, use active voice and avoid long, convoluted sentences. A method comment should state what the method does, its arguments, its effects, and its output.

Prefer

```
"Active voice"
createShell
    "Create the receiver's shell. Hook the focus callback."
```

over

```
"Passive voice"
createShell
    "The receiver's shell is created. The focus callback is hooked."
```

7.4 Guideline: Include executable comments

Pharo offers executable examples in a comment using the message >>>. Executable examples in comments are super cool because, as the reader, you can execute the code and understand the parameters. In addition, the documentation is always synchronized because tools such as the test runner can check that examples are correct.

```
ProtoObject >> ifNil: nilBlock ifNotNil: ifNotNilBlock
  "If the receiver is not nil, pass it as argument to the
     ifNotNilBlock block
  else execute the nilBlock block "

  "(nil ifNil: [42] ifNotNil: [:o | o + 3 ] ) >>> 42"
  "(3 ifNil: [42] ifNotNil: [:o | o + 3 ]) >>> 6"

  ^ ifNotNilBlock cull: self
```

```
Object >> split: aSequenceableCollection
    "Split the argument using the receiver as a separator."
    "optimized version for single delimiters"
    "($/ split: '/foo/bar')>>>#('' 'foo' 'bar') asOrderedCollection"
    "([:c| c isSeparator] split: 'aa bb cc dd') >>> #('aa' 'bb' 'cc'
        'dd') asOrderedCollection"
```

```
| result |
result := OrderedCollection new: (aSequenceableCollection size / 2)
    asInteger.
self split: aSequenceableCollection do: [ :item |
    result add: item ].
^ result
```

7.5 Guideline: Use CRC-driven class comments

A class is not in isolation, but *implements* responsibilities (mainly one) and *collaborates* with other entities. Therefore a class comment should be composed of at least 3 parts: the class, its responsibilities and how it uses its collaborators. The Class Responsibility Collaboration (CRC) pattern is powerful to design but also to comment classes. Use it for commenting class.

Knowing the instance variables is the least important!

Follow the template given by Pharo that is shown below.

```
Please comment me using the following template inspired by Class
    Responsibility Collaborator (CRC) design:

For the Class part:
  State a one line summary. For example, "I represent a paragraph of
    text".

For the Responsibility part:
  Three sentences about my main responsibilities - what I do, what I
    know.

For the Collaborators Part:
  State my main collaborators and one line about how I interact with
    them.

Public API and Key Messages
    - message one
    - message two
    - (for bonus points) how to create instances.

One simple example is simply gorgeous.

Internal Representation and Key Implementation Points.

Implementation Points
```

7.6 Guideline: Comment the unusual

When a behavior is unusual, performing unexpected actions or using an unexpected algorithm, it is important to comment on it.

In general, comments should make irregular and unusual aspects clearer. You may want to include implementation-dependent or platform specific idiosyncrasies.

CHAPTER 8

Powerful coding idioms

Some coding idioms will make your code a lot clearer. Knowing them is also good because you will code faster.

8.1 Guideline: Do not query twice for the same object

The message `ifNotNil:` expects a block with one argument. This argument is the object that is not nil.

For example,

```
[self doAndReturnThat ifNotNil: [ :that | self doSomethingWith: that ]
```

is better than:

```
| that |
that := self doAndReturnThat.
that ifNotNil: [self doSomethingWith: that]
```

Similarly have a look at the messages containing the `ifPresent:` variations.

```
[aCol at: key ifPresent: [ :present | self doSomethingWith: present]
```

8.2 Guideline: Move return outside branches

When two branches of a condition are returning a value, better move the return out of the blocks.

When two branches of a condition are returning a value, better move the return out of the blocks.

Prefer

```
depth: aNode
    "Returns depth of a tree starting from the given node"
    ...
    ^ leftDepth > rightDepth
        ifTrue: [ 1 + leftDepth ]
        ifFalse: [ 1 + rightDepth ]
```

over

```
depth:aNode
    "Returns depth of a tree starting from the given node"
    ...
    leftDepth > rightDepth
        ifTrue: [ ^ 1 + leftDepth ]
        ifFalse: [ ^ 1 + rightDepth ]
```

8.3   Guideline: Use streamContents

When you want to manipulate a potentially long stream you can avoid to have to define the explicit stream creation and access using `streamContents` with a block whose argument is a ready to use stream.

Prefer

```
[String streamContents: [:s | self displayStringOn: s]
```

over

```
stream := WriteStream on: (String new: 1000).
stream ...
^ stream contents
```

8.4   Guideline: Preallocate overly large collections

You may work on really large collections, and in such a case, the allocation of the collection can have a speed penalty.

If you know in advance how large your collection will be, preallocate a big one and store elements in it:

```
| list |
list := OrderedCollection new: 10000.
1 to: 10000 do: [ :i |
    list add: i ]
```

You can use the method bench to get a first idea.

```
[| list |
list := OrderedCollection new: 100000.
1 to: 100000 do: [ :i |
   list add: i ] ] bench
"for 100,000 get 165.901 per second"
"for 10,000 get 5484.903 per second"

[| list |
list := OrderedCollection new.
1 to: 100000 do: [ :i |
   list add: i ] ] bench
"for 100,000 get 79.368 per second"
"for 10,000 get 5278.544 per second"
```

8.5 Guideline: Use super to send a message with the same selector

super is used to start the method lookup in the superclass of the class of the method containing super. However, super is only necessary when the method you want to invoke has the same than the current one since using self in such a case simply creates and infinite loop.

For example, the following just creates an infinite loop, since the method initialize is calling itself infinitively.

```
initialize

   self initialize.
   self continue
```

This is the only case where you must use super to invoke a method that cannot be reached by the method lookup when it starts from the class defining the method. The correct definition is then:

```
initialize

   super initialize.
   self continue
```

Now there is no need to use super for messages that have a different selector than the method they belong to. For example, there is no need to use super bar in the following, since the defining method is called foo and you send the message bar.

```
foo
   super bar.
   self continue
```

The correct definition is just to use `self`.

```
foo
    self bar.
    self continue
```

While using `super` often does not break your code, it may because if you have a method named `bar` in the same class this method will not be invoked. Always be cautious when reading or writing such code.

CHAPTER 9

Object initialization

One key responsibility for a class is to correctly initialize the instance it creates. This avoids placing the burden on clients of such objects. In this chapter, we will present some patterns to initialize objects.

9.1 Guideline: Take advantage of automatic object initialization

By default Pharo offers a way to initialize your objects. The method `initialize` is automatically sent by the method `new`.

Imagine that we implement a game and that this game needs to initialize the number of turns it plays. Avoid forcing the clients of the game to have the responsibility of initializing the turn. Indeed, if the clients forget to send the expression `turn:`, the game logic may be simply broken.

```
Game new turn: 0
```

Therefore, when you want to initialize the state of your object, simply redefine

```
Game >> initialize
    super initialize.
    turn := 0.
```

This way `Game new` will automatically set the value for `turn`.

From a test perspective, it is often a good practice to have a test covering the default initialization.

```
GameTest >> testDefaultInitialization

  self assert: Game new turn equals: 0
```

9.2 Guideline: No automatic initialize

When you do not want to get the automatic initialization to happen you should use the message `basicNew` on the class side and create your own `initialize-Something:` method.

Let us imagine that the computation of the tiles of a game would be costly or that there would be no simple default. We can propose a class creation interface whose responsibility is to request the mandatory information and initialize only what is needed for the object creation.

Here we define a class method `tileNumber:`, and we do not invoke `new` but `basicNew`. Indeed `new` sends the message `initialize` and we do not want to pay the price for it. `basicNew` just allocates the new object and does not perform any other operations.

```
Game class >> tileNumber: aNumber
  ^ self basicNew
    initializeTiles: aNumber ;
    yourself
```

Now on the instance side we can define the initialization of tiles as shown by the method `initializeTiles:`.

```
Game >> initializeTiles: aNumber
  tiles := Array new: aNumber
```

If you use `new` instead of `basicNew` in previous definition, the `initialize` method and the method `initializeTiles:` will be executed.

9.3 Guideline: No double super new initialize

Since Pharo is automatically sending the message `initialize` as part of the object creation process using the pattern below, there is no need for the developer to do it in addition.

Now you may wonder what the problem is if you inadvertently redefine `new` in one of your classes as follows:

```
Game class >> new

  ^ super new initialize
```

In Pharo, the method `initialize` of the class `Game` will be invoked twice.

9.4 Guideline: initialize does not need to return super

The method `initialize` is a method that modifies the receiver. It is used by convention to initialize the default value of the receiver. It is invoked by default by the message `new`

The following definition is not idiomatic:

```
initialize

    default := 'no'.
    ^ super initialize
```

First it returns a value and this value is not really used. Prefer the following definition:

```
initialize

    default := 'no'.
    super initialize
```

Second, the ordering implies that the first local information should be computed, then one of the superclasses. It may happen that you need this order, but it is rare, so prefer the following canonical form:

```
initialize

    super initialize
    default := 'no'.
```

CHAPTER 10

Potential traps: A syntactic perspective

Understanding possible mistakes is a nice way to avoid them or to spot errors made in your code. Here are some common mistakes.

10.1 Guideline: Use parentheses to disambiguate messages with the same priority

For keyword-messages

The Pharo compiler does not know where to cut an expression composed on multiple keyword-based messages. For example, assert:includes: in the expression `self assert: uUMLClass variables includes: 'name'` can be a message that the object `self` can understand. For example testcases understand the message `assert:equals:` and the following expression is fully valid: `self assert: uUMLClass variables equals: 'name'`.

Therefore, this is the programmer responsibility to use parenthese to separate correctly the messages having the same priority. The following example illustrates this point.

```
testDefineASimpleClass

    | uUMLClass |
    uUMLClass := UMLClass named: 'ComixSerie'.
    uUMLClass instVar: 'name'.
```

```
self assert: uUMLClass variables includes: 'name'
```

There is no message `assert:includes:`. The expression `uUMLClass variables includes: 'name'` should be parenthesized, because this is the result of the execution of this expression that should be passed as argument of the message `assert:`.

```
testDefineASimpleClass

    | uUMLClass |
    uUMLClass := UMLClass named: 'ComixSerie'.
    uUMLClass instVar: 'name'.
    self assert: (uUMLClass variables includes: 'name')
```

Between binary messages

Pharo does not make any assumption about the possible mathematical meaning of messages. As a programmer you cannot describe the weight of a binary messages. It means that in an expression composed of multiple binary messages, they will be executed from left to right.

For example `1 + 2 * 3` returns 9 since first the message plus is resolved and its result is the receiver of the message `*`.

```
1 + 2 * 3
>>> 9
```

To get the correct mathematical behavior, one should use parentheses.

```
1 + (2 * 3)
>>> 7
```

10.2 Guideline: no need for extra parentheses

There is no need for parentheses surrounding unary message. There is not much benefit to add parentheses around unaray messages. In Pharo unary messages are the messages that have the highest priority. They are executed first.

Prefer

```
xMatrix := PMMatrix rows: x asArrayOfRows.
```

over

```
xMatrix := PMMatrix rows: ( x asArrayOfRows ).
```

10.2 Guideline: no need for extra parentheses

No parentheses around message with higher priority

In the similar way, there is no need to put parentheses around binary messages involved in keyword-based expressions. Binary messages are executed prior to keyword-messages. In the following = is executed before ifTrue:.

Prefer
```
reducedX do: [ :row |
  (row at: 'target') = 'Iris-setosa'
    ifTrue: [ a add: row asArray ] ].
```

over
```
reducedX do: [ :row |
  ( (row at: 'target') = 'Iris-setosa' )
    ifTrue: [ a add: (row asArray) ] ].
```

Prefer
```
depth: aNode
  "Returns depth of a tree starting from the given node"

  | leftDepth rightDepth |
  leftDepth := -1.
  aNode leftChild isNotNil
    ifTrue: [ leftDepth := self depth: aNode leftChild ].
  rightDepth := -1.
  aNode rightChild isNotNil
    ifTrue: [ rightDepth := self depth: aNode rightChild ].
  ^ leftDepth > rightDepth
    ifTrue: [ 1 + leftDepth ]
    ifFalse: [ 1 + rightDepth ]
```

over
```
depth:aNode
  "Returns depth of a tree starting from the given node"
  | leftDepth rightDepth |
  leftDepth := -1.
  aNode leftChild isNotNil
  ifTrue: [ leftDepth := self depth: (aNode leftChild) ].
  rightDepth := -1.
  aNode rightChild isNotNil
  ifTrue: [ rightDepth := self depth: (aNode rightChild) ].

  ( leftDepth > rightDepth )
  ifTrue: [ ^ (1 + leftDepth) ]
  ifFalse: [^ (1 + rightDepth ) ].
```

Potential traps: A syntactic perspective

No parentheses around variable

Putting parentheses around a variable does not produce an array, it has no effect. Do not confuse parentheses and curly braces. Curly braces is a shortcut to produce an array with the elements they surround: { a } produces an array with one element whose value is the value held by the variable a as shown by the examples below.

In this code snippet, {} creates an array.

```
| a |
a := 12.
{a} printString
>>> #(12)
```

In this snippet, the parentheses do not do anything.

```
| a |
a := 12.
(a) printString
>>> 12
```

No parentheses around single message

There is no need to put extra parentheses over a single message. It has no effect. Parentheses make sense to disambiguate one message over a set of messages composing an expression.

Prefer

```
m := pca transform: xMatrix
```

over

```
m := (pca transform: xMatrix)
```

10.3 Guideline: receiver of ifTrue:ifFalse: is a boolean

Do not use a block as receiver of a ifTrue:, ifFalse:, ifTrue:ifFalse: or ifFalse:ifTrue: messages.

The following expression is the following:

```
lastNode = 0
  ifTrue:[ lastNode := curNode ]
  ifFalse:[ lastNode next: curNode ]
```

The following expressions do not work

```
[lastNode =0] value
   ifTrue:[ lastNode := curNode ]
   ifFalse:[ lastNode next: curNode ]
```

```
[lastNode =0]
   ifTrue:[ lastNode := curNode ]
   ifFalse:[ lastNode next: curNode ]
```

10.4 Guideline: receiver of whileTrue: is a block

The receiver of the message `whileTrue:` is a block, and its argument is, too.

The following line is incorrect:

```
[ (number < limit) whileTrue: [ do something ]
```

The following line is correct:

```
[ [ number < limit ] whileTrue: [ do something ]
```

10.5 Guideline: Use a Block when you do not know execution time

Often newcomers get confused about when to use ( ) and [ ]. A good way to understand is that we should use [ ] when we do know whether an expression will be executed (may be multiple times).

ifTrue:ifFalse:

The conditional is always executed, while each of the arguments is a block because we do not know which ones will be executed.

```
lastNode = 0
   ifTrue: [ lastNode := curNode ]
   ifFalse: [ lastNode next: curNode ]
```

timesRepeat:

`timesRepeat:`'s argument is a block because we do not know how many times it will be executed.

```
[n timesRepeat: [ lastNode := curNode next ]
```

do:/collect:

The argument of iterators such as do:, collect:,... is a block because we do not know how many times (if any) the block will be executed.

```
[ aCol do: [ :node | ...]
```

10.6 Guideline: Avoid , when in loop

In Pharo string concatenations are expressed using the message #,.

```
'Pharo' , ' with Style'
>>> 'Pharo with Style'
```

The implementation of the method is however not really efficient since it copies the underlying collection during each concatenation as we show below. The alternative is to use a write stream or to use streamContents: but using a stream makes the code more complex. Therefore there is a key question to be answered: When is it pointless to use a WriteStream and just use #, ?

Avoid #, when the code is in a loop or recursion, use a stream.

```
[ String streamContents: [:s | 1 to: 10000 do: [ :i | s << i asString ]]
```

Use #, when constructing error messages, class initialisation code, or situations where there is no loop.

Note that in printOn: methods, the argument is already a stream so we use it and avoid using message #,.

Difference in speed

The following snippets shows the difference in execution on large concatenations.

```
[ String streamContents: [:s | 1 to: 10000 do: [ :i | s << i asString
    ]] ] bench
>>> '551.890 per second'
```

```
[ | s |
    s := ''.
    1 to: 10000 do: [ :i | s := s, i asString ] ] bench
>>> '8.465 per second'
```

```
[ String streamContents: [:s | 1 to: 1000 do: [ :i | s << i asString
    ]]  ] bench
>>> '6313.137 per second'
```

```
[ | s |
    s := ''.
    1 to: 1000 do: [ :i | s := s, i asString ] ] bench
>>> '967.819 per second'
```

10.7 Guideline: super is just self

super is the receiver of the message, just as self. No super is not the superclass, nor an instance of the superclass. super is the receiver of the message.

There is no need to use super when returning an expression not passing it as argument. For example passing super as argument is useless and show that the developer did fully get what super it.

```
foo

    anotherObject bar: super.
    self continue.
```

Better use self

```
foo

    anotherObject bar: self.
    self continue.
```

Similarly

```
foo
    ^ super
```

Better use self

```
foo
    ^ self
```

10.8 Guideline: Do not reuse temporaries

Readable code is key and reusing a local temporary variable to store different objects during the execution of a method should be avoided. Creating a separate temporary does not incur any execution cost. Therefore, create a temporary variable instead of storing different objects inside the same variable at different execution points of a method.

10.9 Guideline: Do not change behavior of well-known messages

When reading code, developers read it in the context of core libraries, a common vocabulary, and expected behavior. Therefore, it is important not to define methods having the same name as a common message but that exhibit different behaviors.

When you define a method, you can check really fast using implementors if existing libraries have already defined such a message.

10.10 Guideline: Use iterators

Pharo has a large collection of really powerful iterators in its deep core. Use `do:`, `collect:`, `select:`, `reject:` to start with.

Prefer

`[collection do: [ :element | ... ]`

over

`[1 to: collection size do: [ :index | ... ]`

This is the only case where you must use `super` to invoke the method that cannot be reach by the method lookup when it starts from the class defining the method. The correct definition is then:

10.11 Guideline: Avoid low-level messages

Pharo offers a large set of low-level messages such as `isKindOf:`, `isMemberOf:`, `become:`, `canUnderstand:`, `doesNotUnderstand:`, ... Such messages are handy for constructing tools and the infrastructure of the language. However, such methods make the code more complex and often more fragile. In addition, some are more costly and, in addition, break basic cross-references. So, always consider whether such methods are truly necessary.

10.12 Guideline: Do not abuse blocks

Blocks are powerful. They are handy because they are like anonymous methods created on the fly. Avoid nest blocks and complex flow when explicit methods are possible.

Prefer

10.13 Guideline: Do not write lengthly blocks

```
action1
   ... code1

action2
   ... code2

some method
   x <y
      ifTrue: [ self action1 ]
      ifFasel: [ self action2 ]
```

over
```
action1 := [ ... code1 ].
action2 := [ ... code2 ]

some method
   x <y
      ifTrue: [ action1 value ]
      ifFasel: [ action2 value ]
```

10.13 Guideline: Do not write lengthly blocks

Now, writing long blocks is a problem because blocks are not methods and you cannot simply call them. In addition, blocks do not create simple hook methods that subclasses can customize.

A good practice is to keep the block body length short and to convert long blocks into methods and call such methods from the block.

Prefer
```
messageWithBlock
   body of a long block

anObject use: [ self messageWithBlock ]
```

over
```
anObject use: [ ... body of a long block ... ]
```

10.14 Guideline: Exception catch MUST not be empty

Exceptional behavior can be captured and controlled using on:do:. Now this is important not to catch an exceptional behavior and do nothing. This is basically the worst thing you can do, and it will backfire on you months later. In addition, it makes your code super difficult to debug.

Prefer

```
[ expression ] on: Error do: [:ex | Stdio stderr nextPutAll: 'Error
    in...' ]
```

over

```
[ expression ] on: Error do: []
```

CHAPTER 11

Potential traps: About `printing` and Streams

Stream usage in the case of printing objects may be sometimes confusing. In this chapter we clarify some of pitfalls.

11.1 Guideline: `printString` vs. `displayString`

Newcomers are often confused between `printString` and `displayString` and their counterparts `printOn:` and `displayStringOn::`.

- `printString` is used for debugging, that's why the default implementation shows the class name. It's implemented by specializing `printOn:` on your classes.
- `displayString` is used for nicely display objects in list. It is implemented by specializing `displayStringOn:` on your classes.

If you have aPerson:

```
aPerson printString
>>> 'aPerson (''John Doe'')'
```

```
aPerson displayString
>>> 'John Doe'
```

11.2 Guideline: About `printString`

Let us take a moment to step back about stream usage in `printOn:` methods. The `printString` method creates a stream and passes this stream as argument of the `printOn:` method as shown below:

```
Object >> printString
  "Answer a String whose characters are a description of the receiver.
  If you want to print without a character limit, use fullPrintString."

  ^ self printStringLimitedTo: 50000
```

```
Object >> printStringLimitedTo: limit
  "Answer a String whose characters are a description of the receiver.
  If you want to print without a character limit, use fullPrintString."

  ^self printStringLimitedTo: limit using: [:s | self printOn: s]
```

```
Object >> printStringLimitedTo: limit using: printBlock
  "Answer a String whose characters are a description of the receiver
  produced by given printBlock. It ensures the result will be not
    bigger than given limit"

  | limitedString |
  limitedString := String streamContents: printBlock limitedTo: limit.
  limitedString size < limit ifTrue: [^ limitedString].
  ^ limitedString , '...etc...'
```

What you should see is that the method `printStringLimitedTo:using:` is creating a stream and passing it around.

When you redefine the method `printOn:` in your class, if you send the message `printString` on the instance variables of your object, you are in fact creating yet another stream and copying its contents in the first one.

Here is an example:

```
MessageTally >> displayStringOn: aStream
  self displayIdentifierOn: aStream.
  aStream
    nextPutAll: ' (';
    nextPutAll: self tally printString;
    nextPutAll: ')'
```

This is clearly counterproductive. It is much better to send the message `print:` to the stream or `printOn:` to the instance variable it as follows:

11.3 Guideline: Unnecessary stream creation

```
MessageTally >> displayStringOn: aStream
  self displayIdentifierOn: aStream.
  aStream
    nextPutAll: ' (';
    print: self tally;
    nextPutAll: ')'
```

To understand what the method `print:`, here its definition:

```
Stream >> print: anObject
  "Have anObject print itself on the receiver."

  anObject printOn: self
```

Pay attention, sending the `printString` message is often wrong and it is the duties of the system to do it.

11.3 Guideline: Unnecessary stream creation

Unnecessary stream creation can happen in other situations than `printString`. Here is an example taken from Pharo.

```
printProtocol: protocol sourceCode: sourceCode

  ^ String streamContents: [ :stream |
    stream
      nextPutAll: '"protocol: ';
      nextPutAll: protocol printString;
      nextPut: $"; cr; cr;
      nextPutAll: sourceCode ]
```

What you should see is that a stream is created and then another stream is created and discarded with the expression `protocol printString`. A better implementation is the following using `print:`.

```
printProtocol: protocol sourceCode: sourceCode

  ^ String streamContents: [ :stream |
    stream
      nextPutAll: '"protocol: ';
      print: protocol;
      nextPut: $"; cr; cr;
      nextPutAll: sourceCode ]
```

11.4 Guideline: `printString` vs. `asString`

Another difficulty you may encounter is to see the difference between `printString` and `asString`.

- `printString` is used for debugging, that's why the default implementation shows the class name. It's implemented by specializing `printOn:` on your classes.
- `asString` converts an object into a string. It is equivalent to the `toString()` in other languages.

Let us take an example with the symbol `#foo`.

Printing the symbol `#foo` is just printing it as symbol.

```
#foo printString
>>> '#foo'
```

Sending the message `asString` to the symbol `#foo` converts it to a string.

```
#foo asString
>>> 'foo'
```

The situation is the same for strings but it can be a bit more destabilizing. The conversion of a string to a string is the string itself.

```
'foo' asString
>>> 'foo'
```

Now printing a string includes the quotes and quotes should be double quoted.

```
'foo' printString
>>> '''foo'''
```

CHAPTER 12

Use Patterns

In this chapter we present some points about existing libraries or functionality that are often misunderstood and lead to code of lesser quality.

12.1 Guideline: Write small methods

Long methods are a sign of less mature code. Indeed, small methods offer many strong advantages:

- Are easier to read and understand,
- Are easier to test,
- Are easier to reuse and compose,
- Are elementary pieces of customization. Indeed, sending a message to self creates a hook that subclasses can customize within their context. This is the foundation of object-oriented programming.

As measured by Zaitsev and Ducasse, Pharo methods (excluding test methods) have 3 lines of code as a median value. Therefore, this is not just anecdotal but an important point.

12.2 Guideline: Avoid singletons

Singletons are evil because they make you feel that you are writing object-oriented code, but in reality they are disguised global variables. Now you can ask yourself why this would be a problem.

This is a problem when you want to modularize your code. In essence, you cannot substitute a singleton with another object, and any change to the singleton is widely visible.

A symptom of the problem is when you want to write tests. You often do not want to have your tests impact the complete system. So think twice before using a singleton.

A good way to know if you need a singleton is whether you can add an instance variable to your domain objects and pass a reference to the object that you would like to have as a singleton. If you can avoid the singleton just with the addition of an instance variable, it means that you did not need the singleton.

This is why good object-oriented designers say that Singleton is about time and not space, meaning that you need a singleton when you cannot have two instances working at the same time - Think about a scheduler. You cannot have two scheduler manipulating threads at the same time.

The following guideline is an example of a Singleton bad use.

12.3 Guideline: Avoid explicit Transcript

We present why `Transcript` can be really badly used. We present that with some simple care we can develop modular solutions that are flexible and can take advantages of using `Transcript` without the inconvenients. Let us imagine that you still want to log strings.

First simple case

`Transcript` is a kind of stdout on which you can write some strings outputs. It is cheap. The class exposes a stream-based API (and this is a really important design point as we will see in the future).

Here is a typical not really good use of `Transcript`

```
myMethod
    Transcript show: 'foo' ; cr
```

It is not really good because it hardcodes a reference to `Transcript` while Pharo proposes some helpers methods such as `traceCr:`.

```
myMethod
    self traceCr: 'foo'
```

Some developers may think that this is not important but it can help you if one day you want to control the logging and for example use an object with the same API but to do something else. So avoid hardcoding globals. But there is more.

12.4 The real concern

The problem amongst others is that Transcript is a singleton and in fact a global variable. Once you use it for real in your code, you basically killed the modularity of your program and the only thing that you can do is to hope that nothing bad can happen.

Let us look at a concrete simple case. The microdown Parser came (yes we removed this) with a simple method named closeMe:

```
MicAbstractBlock >> closeMe

    Transcript << 'Closing ' << self class name; cr; endEntry
```

So this method is producing a little trace so that the parser developer could understand what was happening. So you can think that this is ok.

There are two main problems:

- First what if you want to deploy your application in a system where you do not want at all to get Transcript its class and all its family. Think for example about people producing minimal images.
- Second, when Pharo is built on Jenkins all the tests are executed because we love tests. And this Transcript expression produces dirt on the build log. You do not want to have read such a trace when you are trying to understand why the build is not working.

```
Closing MicCodeBlock
Closing MicCodeBlock
Closing MicCodeBlock
Closing MicCodeBlock
Closing MicCodeBlock
Closing MicCodeBlock
Closing MicCodeBlock
Closing MicCodeBlock
Closing MicHeaderBlock
Closing MicHeaderBlock
Closing MicHeaderBlock
Closing MicHeaderBlock
Closing MicListItemBlock
Closing MicListItemBlock
Closing MicOrderedListBlock
```

Now let us see the good way to have a log and be able to unplug it.

12.5 Guideline: Parametrized your object with log stream

The solution is really simple. Just use object-oriented programming and encapsulation. To support the Parser developer, we can simply add a stream to the class.

For example we define a new variable to and initialize it to a write stream.

```
Object subclass: #MicAbstractBlock
  instanceVariableNames: 'parent children parser logStream'
  classVariableNames: ''
  package: 'Microdown-Model'
```

```
MicAbstractBlock >> initialize
  super initialize.
  children := OrderedCollection new.
   logStream := WriteStream on: (String new: 1000)
```

Then we can rewrite the method `closeMe` as follows

```
MicAbstractBlock >> closeMe
  logStream << 'Closing ' << self class name; cr
```

Then we can provide a simple setter method so that the developer can set for example the Transcript as a stream to write to.

```
MicAbstractBlock >> logStream: aStream
  logStream := aStream
```

12.6 When instance creation is delicate

If we do not control the creation of instances of the class using the stream, we will have difficulties configuring it with the correct stream. So if you want to be able to configure the class to use a different logger, we should define a class variable so that we can send message to the class and at initialization time, we can take the value from the class variable instead of hardcoding the WriteStream.

Here is a sketch to illustrate the idea.

We add a class variable `DefaultStream` to the class.

```
Object subclass: #MicAbstractBlock
  instanceVariableNames: 'parent children parser logStream'
  classVariableNames: 'DefaultStream'
  package: 'Microdown-Model'
```

12.6 When instance creation is delicate

We define one setter. This is using this setter that we will be able to say to the system that for a given execution it should write to the `Transcript`: for example doing `MicAbstractBlock logStream: Transcript`.

```
MicAbstractBlock class >> logStream: aStream
  DefaultStream := aStream
```

We make sure that the class variable is initialized to a default stream. Now we do it in way that we can later reset the stream to such default stream.

```
MicAbstractBlock class >> reset
  self logStream: (WriteStream on: (String new: 1000))
```

Here we hardcode the stream and alternate solution that extract this expression in a separate messages if it makes sense for subclass to specialize.

```
MicAbstractBlock class >> initialize
  self reset
```

And we will be able to reset the default solution either by reinitializing the class `MicAbstractBlock initialize` or `MicAbstractBlock logStream: MicAbstractBlock defaultValueForStream`

Now we make sure that the instance creation uses the default stream hold by the class.

```
MicAbstractBlock >> initialize
  super initialize.
  children := OrderedCollection new.
   logStream := DefaultStream
```

The net result is that we have control and can decide what is happening. In addition, we can write tests to make sure that the logging is correct. Because using Transcript makes this a brittle exercise since someone else may write to the Transcript when you do not expect it.

Conclusion

`Transcript` is not bad per se. But it promotes bad coding practices. Developers should stop listening to the sirens of easy and cheap global variables. With a little bit of care and a limited infrastructure, it is possible to get the best of both worlds: modular objects and taking advantage of the existing infrastructure whose `Transcript` belongs to.

What we presented about `Transcript` can be applied to any global object or singleton. This is not because a library exposes a singleton that you have to blindly use. You should apply sound principles and protect yourself from the impact of changes.

12.7 Guideline: Wrap explicit signal raising

One question that you can ask yourself is which one of the two following situations is the best:

- Case one. Using the expression `self error: 'Oh no!'` and defining the method `error:` in your class (or calling)
- Case two. Using the expression `Error signal: 'Oh no!'`

The case one is better. As general principle, defining a method and sending a message is often better because sending self-send messages create hooks that your subclasses can take advantage of.

For example imagine the following situation

```
MyClass >> ohNoError
    Error signal: 'Oh no!'
```

```
MyClass >> ohNoErrorUser
    x isSomethingBad
        ifTrue: [ self error: 'Oh no!' ]
```

Then you can redefine `ohNoError` in your subclass.

```
MyClassSubclass >> ohNoError
    Error signal: 'Oh no! Really no!'
```

CHAPTER 13

Conclusion

We hope that you enjoyed this guideline list. Remember that you write code once and will read it a thousand times. Take the time to give good names. However, finding good names is not an easy task, but you can use refactorings to improve things easily.

This goes in pairs with tests.

You write a test once and it gets executed a million times. Therefore, write tests to exercise the names you use and change them until they help you tell stories that can be understood.